Power of Poetry

Writing Activities to Spark Creative Thinking

Joan Groeber

Illustrated by Terry Sirrell

Rigby Best Teachers Press

An imprint of Rigby

For more information about other books from Rigby Best Teachers Press, please contact Rigby at 1-800-822-8661 or visit **www.rigby.com.**

Editor: Julia Moses
Executive Editor: Laura Strom
Designer: Street Level Studio
Design Project Manager: Tom Sjoerdsma
Illustrator: Terry Sirrell

06 05 04 03 02
10 9 8 7 6 5 4 3 2

Printed in the United States of America.

ISBN 0-7635-7562-3
The Power of Poetry

Table of Contents

Introduction 1

References 2

How to Use This Book 3

Section 1: PRESENTING AND SHARING POETRY IN THE CLASSROOM 4

Poetry Inventory *What Do You Think?* 5

Poetry *Do* List: *Top 10 Tips for Teaching Poetry* 6

Poetry *Don't* List: *Poetry Pitfalls* 7

Poetry and the Writing Process 8

Creating a Poetry-Friendly Classroom 10

Poetic Devices 12

Section 2: EXPERIMENTING WITH FORMULA AND WORD-COUNT POEMS 15

A Note About Using This Section 16

Acrostic Background 17

Acrostic Whole Group 18

Acrostic Independent 19

Cinquain Background 20

Cinquain Whole Group 21

Cinquain Independent 22

Clerihew Background 23

Clerihew Whole Group 24

Clerihew Independent 25

Concrete Background 26

Concrete Whole Group 27

Concrete Independent 28

Diamante Background 29

Diamante Whole Group 30

Diamante Independent 31

Found Background 32

Found Whole Group 33

Found Independent 34

Haiku Background 35

Haiku Whole Group 36

Haiku Independent 37

Table of Contents

Limerick Background 38

Limerick Whole Group 39

Limerick Independent 40

Tanka Background 41

Tanka Whole Group 42

Tanka Independent 43

Sonnet Background 44

Sonnet Whole Group 46

Ballad Background 47

Ballad Whole Group 50

Section 3: USING POETRY ACROSS THE CURRICULUM

Section 3: USING POETRY ACROSS THE CURRICULUM 52

The Shape of Things to Come: Science 53

From A to Z: Science 54

Nature's Diamonds: Science 55

Sing a Song of Science: Science 56

Who Am I?: Social Studies 57

The Ballad of a Famous Person: Social Studies 58

It's a Celebration!: Social Studies 59

"A" is for America: Social Studies 60

Amos, the Alliterative Alligator: Language Arts/Spelling 61

Dear Poet: Creative Writing 62

Character Study: Literature/Language Arts 63

Scenes from a Poem: Art 64

Section 4: INSTANT POETRY

Section 4: INSTANT POETRY 65

Riddle Rhyme 66

Introducing the One and Only 67

Hilarious Homograph-a-phones 68

It's Time to Rhyme 69

A Clerihew for You 70

Think Hink-Pink 71

Diamante for Two 72

Color Me a Rainbow 73

Tomorrow and Today 74

Being Me 75

Bibliography 76

Poetry is a valuable learning resource. It is through this lyrical language that learners of all ages may come to know more about themselves and others. The study of any literary form, including poetry, must begin with the presentation of examples for learners to hear and see prior to the time when they will be invited to create and share their own works. Because the basis for learning anything new is modeling and exposure, a reference list of poetry anthologies is provided on the following page. This list is in no way exhaustive. Your local library or bookstore is a treasure trove of marvelous anthologies. You will also find poetry on the Internet and many sites have poems to print out for use in a classroom.

The more students are exposed to poetry of all kinds, the more likely they are to develop not only a meaningful connection to it, but an ability to compose their own poems as well. While not every student will have an equal understanding or love of poetry, the opportunity to read and write poems remains an essential component in their intellectual and aesthetic development.

The study of poetry provides a wonderful opportunity for students and teachers to use their five senses as they reach out to the physical world. Some of the most effective lessons are developed around exercises that encourage the students to collect sensory information while experiencing a place or thing and sharing their reactions with others through poetry. The economy of words and depth of expression associated with poetry makes it a natural choice for student authors who wish to reflect on their private selves. Using words and phrases, students are able to carve powerful images that embody fears, dreams, and feelings about life and their place in this world.

References

The Power of Poetry provides a wide variety of ways to bring poetry to life for students by finding examples of its rhythm, rhyme, and imagery in everyday life. This real-world connection fosters a greater understanding for students who process information in an analytical manner and need to see where poetry fits from a more universal perspective.

The word *anthology* comes from the Greek words *anthos* and *logia,* which mean flower gathering. Think of a poetry anthology as the gathering of flowers.

There are, of course, many fabulous books of poetry by a single author. Shel Silverstein has long been a favorite of many children and his works can be a wonderful addition to your classroom library. However, anthologies bring to your class the richness of many authors and forms in one book—the beauty of many flowers. The following is a list of popular children's anthologies.

The Oxford Book of Story Poems, Oxford University Press.

The Oxford Treasury of Children's Poems, Oxford University Press.

The Random House Book of Poetry for Children, Selected by Jack Prelutsky Random House.

The 20th Century Children's Poetry Treasury, Selected by Jack Prelutsky Alfred A. Knopf.

Lots of Limericks, Selected by Myra Cohn Livingston Margaret K. McElderly Books.

The Oxford Book of Children's Verse in America, Chosen and Edited by Donald Hall Oxford University Press.

Kids Pick the Funniest Poems, Selected by Bruce Lansky Simon and Schuster.

Kingfisher Book of Children's Poetry, Selected by Mark Rosen Kingfisher.

Ten-Second Rainshowers: Poems by Young People, Compiled by Sandford Lyne Simon and Schuster.

Side by Side Poems to Read Together, Collected by Lee Bennett Hopkins Simon and Schuster.

Poetry for Young People, (series)
Robert Louis Stevenson
Edgar Allan Poe
Henry Wadsworth Longfellow
Emily Dickinson
Sterling Publishing Company.

This book is divided into four sections:

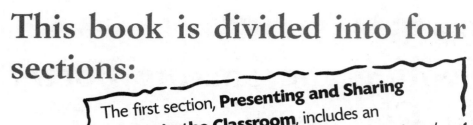

The first section, **Presenting and Sharing Poetry in the Classroom**, includes an inventory to help you understand your students' perceptions of poetry. Separate *do* and *don't* lists are provided to guide you in maximizing the benefits of exploring poetry. An overview of the poetry-writing process is included, as well as tips for a poetry-friendly environment and brief explanations of poetic elements.

The second section, **Experimenting with Formula and Word-Count Poems**, includes reproducible pages for using formula poems, which allows students to experiment with a variety of styles.

The third section, **Using Poetry Across the Curriculum**, has a number of suggested activities for incorporating poetry writing across the curriculum.

The final section titled **Instant Poetry** offers easy, ready-to-use ideas that will get and keep students interested in the study of poetry.

Section 1:
Presenting and Sharing Poetry in the Classroom

Discovering and exploring the world of poetry can be an exciting and rewarding journey for students. Many students arrive in the classroom with preconceived notions about what to expect from a poetry lesson. These opinions are often based solely on what they have heard, rather than experienced first-hand. Breaking down the stereotypes surrounding the study and composition of poetry is one of the first obstacles to overcome in planning and implementing a successful unit of study.

As with any topic, before moving forward with specific activities and lessons, it is a good idea to determine and assess student background knowledge regarding poetry. This informal inventory can include questions regarding previous exposure to poetry, current opinions concerning poetry, favorite poems or poets, and any expectations regarding the upcoming unit in class. This information can save time and duplication of effort in designing exercises for a specific student population.

Poetry Inventory

Think about what you already know or feel about poetry to complete these phrases.

Reading (or hearing) poetry makes me feel _____

because _____

My favorite subject to write poems about is _____

because _____

While writing a poem, I like to _____

because _____

My favorite kind of poem (or favorite poet) is _____

because _____

One kind of poetry I really don't like is _____

because _____

The best poem anyone ever read to me is _____

I liked it because _____

I think that reading and writing poetry this year in school will be _____

because _____

Poetry *Do* List

1. **Do** read poetry aloud and encourage students to do the same.

2. **Do** provide opportunities for students to share their poems with others.

3. **Do** promote poetry as a valuable means of self-expression.

4. **Do** demonstrate a positive attitude about reading and writing poetry.

5. **Do** experiment with reading and writing different types of poetry.

6. **Do** collect and share the works of several popular children's poets.

7. **Do** encourage students to write poetry on topics that interest them.

8. **Do** arrange for students to correspond (if possible) with their favorite poets.

9. **Do** write and share your own poetry with the community of student poets.

10. **Do** stress the importance of a poem's content over grammatical correctness.

Poetry *Don't* List

1. **Don't** over-analyze the elements or theme of poems.

2. **Don't** require random memorization of lengthy or complicated poetry.

3. **Don't** insist that student poems *always* rhyme or follow a specific formula.

4. **Don't** assume that all students will enjoy poetry before *or* after exposure to it.

5. **Don't** force students to share *every* poem they write with the class.

6. **Don't** relegate poetry class to a Friday afternoon or indoor recess activity.

7. **Don't** project a negative attitude about poetry or poets.

8. **Don't** restrict potential poetry topics to upbeat or positive themes.

9. **Don't** share the content of student poetry without that student's permission.

10. **Don't** underestimate students' ability to create meaningful poems.

Poetry and the Writing Process

Poetry is a craft in which the first impressions of the poet are the most important. Think of a poem as a photograph with words. The poem should capture the moment and be appreciated later. That is why too much emphasis on a process for writing poems can sometimes limit students' creativity. After adequate exposure to a variety of poetry and explicit instruction about a poem's form, students must be able to try for themselves. Allow for approximations and realize that the structure of a poem, limited by word or syllable count, is not as important as students' words expressed creatively.

Prewriting

As with any form of writing, pre-writing is essential. It helps get those fragile ideas down on paper. Once a key word or phrase comes to mind, people tend to free-associate. That is, they think of all the words that they personally relate to the keyword. Encourage students to write their free associations as a web to organize their thoughts. Traditionally people make lists or outlines to organize their writing. While that works for some forms of writing, it tends to stunt creativity. So allow students to write their ideas all over the page and then draw connections where they see them.

Composing

The next step in the writing process is typically called drafting. However, in poetry this step is simply referred to as writing or composing the poem. If a particular format is being followed, this is where students should begin to pay attention to syllable count and word choice. Allowing students some room outside of the rigid guidelines of a format can go a long way toward their success and ultimately their positive feeling about poetry.

Revising

There are two ways to approach revision. One way is to view a poet's first words as a valuable image and therefore to demand revision would be to lose the significance of a poet's impressions. On the other hand, the purpose of revision is to improve the quality, and no one type of writing is above a second look. It is best to allow the poets themselves to decide if their work could use revision. The bottom line is to always encourage students to look for ways to improve their writing, but requiring them to make specific changes can do more harm than good.

Editing

Editing is an essential part of the writing process. Since poetry does not adhere to the usual grammatical conventions, students can have some freedoms while maintaining a readable piece. Ask students to look for errors that detract from the quality of their poem. Once again, though, it is important that you are not overly rigid.

Publishing

Publishing is the final step of the writing process. Unlike other forms of writing, which can be enjoyed in written form, poetry is meant to be heard due to its rhythm and cadence. For that reason, time should be set aside when the class can listen to the poems of classmates and published authors. Never force a student to share work that they consider too personal to reveal to classmates. Allow them to read the work of a published author instead so that they may experience creating a mood with their voice.

Creating a Poetry-Friendly Classroom

Begin by introducing poetry into your classroom in a way that will not intimidate reluctant poets. Choose friendly, fun poems to read aloud. Read for a few minutes every day without expecting responses from students. This will familiarize students with the way poetry sounds and give the message that, above all, it is meant to be enjoyed.

When the time comes to analyze and compose poems, teachers should be mindful that not only is poetry a valid and meaningful form of self-expression, but also that this worthwhile literary form should be explored in a light-hearted way.

Conduct a walk-through of your classroom. Look for evidence of a positive poetry attitude. Do you have poetry books, tapes, or posters on display? Below you will find ways to create a poetry-friendly environment.

Poetry Library

Students should not be expected to write poetry until they have had an opportunity to read and hear the work of published poets. Fill the class library with examples of poetry and provide time for students to explore.

Writing Center

Celebrate the unique quality of this genre by including specialty papers (various colors and shapes) and writing instruments (markers, pastels, colored pencils) in the student writing area.

Listening Zones

Have students practice a favorite poem and create tape recordings of poems for other students to hear. Use poetry CDs available from bookstores and libraries. Set aside a poet's corner for student authors to share their compositions with classmates.

> "Reading a poem silently instead of saying a poem is like the difference between staring at sheet music and actually humming or playing the music on an instrument."
>
> – Robert Pinsky, Poet Laureate

Poetry Notebooks

Ideas and inspirations can be fragile. For this reason students should have poetry notebooks. Use inexpensive spiral notebooks that students can decorate to make personal. Encourage them to carry the notebooks and write in them often. They can write interesting words they see or hear, a line from a book or poem, perhaps even a sketch of an object they would like to write about. The notebooks should not be used for assessment or sharing. Students' notebooks will become the untidy thought balloons of would-be poets.

Idea Center

Maintain an idea box or bulletin board in which teacher and students can offer suggestions–perhaps a word, a photograph, or even an object–for possible inspiration. When students are unable to think of an idea for their latest poem, they may use an inspiration from the box or bulletin board.

Poetic Devices

In exploring the works of published poets, students may begin to see a unique pattern in the organization of this literary form. Poems are read at a measured pace or cadence and contain more frequent pauses and a wider range of verbal tones than those found in prose. In addition, poetry makes use of specific devices to illustrate comparison, noise, or emphasis on a particular idea. Becoming more familiar with these devices enables the student poets to use them in their own compositions.

Delay labeling these terms until students have had a chance to experience them in real poetry so that they will have a point of reference for the term. When this occurs, discuss the term and look for additional examples of this device in other poems.

Alliteration

When two or more words in a row begin with the same letter you have alliteration. An interesting way to remember this device is to think of it as a succession of similar sounds. It often helps rhyme or rhythm and can have a silly effect.

**Daddy does the dishes
for my mom once in a while
he doesn't really like to,
but it makes my mommy smile.**

Tongue twisters are the superlative form of alliteration. Students usually find writing tongue twisters fun, and it is good practice for alliterating poems.

Simile

This is one of the most common forms of comparison. Simile uses the words *like* or *as* in the statement.

**Quiet as snow I spied
the doe, a fawn by her side
how soft and how lovely
the two standing there,
do they see me?**

Metaphor

This is another device that makes comparisons, but without using *like* or *as*. Metaphor presents a more powerful statement. The words *is*, *are*, and *of* are used most often.

**Freedom is the sea
wide open,
expansive,
traveling as far
as you're willing to go.**

Onomatopoeia

Words that make sounds like the things they represent. (Dr. Seuss' book *Mr. Brown Can Moo! Can You?* is an excellent model).

**Crash, bang,
the cymbals clanged.**

**Puppy jumped on
my lap to lick me
SCHLERP!
now my face is
wet and sticky.**

Personification

This device is used to attribute human qualities and ideas to things. It allows readers/listeners to use their own experience to visualize the inanimate object's movements.

Some examples of personification:

Light danced on golden curls.

Memories tell an impressive tale.

Repetition

The use of a word or line repeated two or more times. This device often takes the form of a song refrain or chant, unifying the other ideas in the poem.

Today's a new day
I greet it anew.
It's fresh and exciting, unspoiled.
Today's a new day
I can't wait to live it.
Possibilities are endless,
I know.
Today's a new day
I'll do my best
to love, learn, think, laugh, and grow.

Rhyme

This common device makes use of words whose final vowel syllables make the same sound. By placing these words at the end of each line the poet creates a desired cadence to the poem as readers/listeners emphasize or pause as they hear the repeated sounds. Assigning letters to the rhyming words helps students see the pattern.

How do you know	a
where an elephant will go	a
if he's always taking his trunk?	b
Don't ask me,	c
I am trying to flee	c
from this persistent skunk.	b

Section 2:
Experimenting with Formula and Word-Count Poems

Beginning student writers may experience some difficulty expressing feelings through poetry. Prior to their introduction to poetic forms, their written work has been organized in a predictable format, as in a letter or report. These forms can be used as a framework for arranging ideas in print. In poetry, however, much of this structure is missing and students are often confused about the length and general organization of their work.

Formula and word count poems represent only one facet of poetry. They do, however, provide the type of structure that eases student writers' transition from basic expository writing to a wide variety of poetic forms. These forms are also more easily adapted into other areas of the curriculum.

Formula poems follow a basic set of directions that, when followed, create a distinct form of poetry, whether it be a limerick, diamante, or an acrostic. While the form of these poems is constant, individual student expressions make each composition unique. In a word-count poem, such as tanka, haiku, or a cinquain, a set number of words or syllables is used to create a specific poetic form. In both instances, student writers should be encouraged to express their ideas as they make use of these poetic frameworks that will hold their words in place.

As students become more comfortable conveying their emotions through poetry, they may still return to some of these forms for future compositions as well as finding other, less structured methods of communication, such as free verse poetry. Nonetheless, their exposure to these forms will deepen their understanding of the way words and phrases are arranged to create the lyrical flow of language that is unique to poetry.

A Note About Using This Section:

In this section you will find 11 types of formula poems, each with teacher pages and a student page.

Background

Background pages are teacher support pages that provide you with information about each type of poetry. Included on the background pages are sample poems and patterns that show syllable count, rhyme, and/or poetic elements.

Whole Group

Whole Group pages can be reproduced as overheads and used for a shared writing activity. These pages provide a sample poem for discussing poetic elements, rhyme, and rhythm. Lines are arranged for composing a whole-class poem. This gives students the opportunity to collaborate on a formula poem before they try it independently.

Independent

Independent pages can be reproduced for students to work independently or in small groups. These pages provide directions for getting started, composing, and revising.

Rigby Best Teachers Press

ACROSTIC
Background

Acrostic style poetry is a form dating back to the ancient Greeks and Romans. It uses a single word, written vertically, as its theme. Each letter represents the first letter of the first word on each line. There are two ways to write an acrostic. One way is to compose a list of attributes that begin with the title letters as in "Waterfalls." The other way is to write a statement or question woven through the title as in "Mother." The purpose of either form is to develop an image related to the theme.

WATERFALLS

Wonderful
Azure
Teardrops
Eluding
Rivers
Free
Alive
Like
Laughing
Spirit

STAR

Sits in
The heavens
Always
Revealing light.

MOTHER

Makes an
Opportunity
To
Hug,
Even for no
Reason

Writing acrostic poetry is relatively easy, and it is a good way for students to learn about choosing the right words. Because we already have a wealth of information about ourselves, our names make excellent subjects for acrostics. On the following page there is a place for students to compose an acrostic about themselves.

Teacher's Tip ☺

Using acrostics as a comparison/contrast activity is an alternative to a Venn diagram.

Whole Group

WATERFALLS

Wonderful
Azure
Teardrops
Eluding
Rivers
Free
Alive
Like
Laughing
Spirit

_____   _____

_____   _____

_____   _____

_____   _____

_____   _____

_____   _____

_____   _____

_____   _____

_____   _____

_____   _____

ACROSTIC
Independent

Before you begin composing an acrostic about yourself, take some time to organize your thoughts. Use the table below to write down information about yourself. Begin by writing in one box words that describe you physically. Then in another box write about your personality. Use the other boxes for likes and dislikes and favorite things. Next think about your family and how you would describe them. Finally, you should think about your hopes and dreams and plans for the future.

Once you have written words and phrases that tell about you, choose those that you feel are most important. If there is a word or phrase that describes you well but doesn't begin with a letter in your name, think of a similar word that will work in your poem.

Write your name on the spaces below. Then compose your acrostic.

CINQUAIN

Background

A *cinquain* is a word-count poem invented in 1911 by Adelaide Crapsey. Cinquains contain 5 lines and 22 syllables, distributed in a specific 2-4-6-8-2 pattern. These poems resemble the Japanese *haiku* and describe a person, place, thing, or activity. It is important to recognize that cinquains do not rhyme but they do flow smoothly. A properly written cinquain will create an image in usually a sentence or two. It should not sound like disconnected words or phrases thrown together for the syllable count. Below are two patterns and examples of cinquains.

Pattern 1

Line 1: one-word, two-syllable subject
Line 2: 4 syllables that describe the subject
Line 3: 6 syllables that express action relating to the subject
Line 4: 8 syllables that express feeling or an observation about the subject
Line 5: 2 syllables that describe or rename the subject

Children
are the laughing
heart of a happy home
the joy, the smiles, and most of all
the love.

Pattern 2

Line 1: one-word subject
Line 2: two descriptive words
Line 3: three action words
Line 4: four words that express feelings relating to the subject
Line 5: a two-word synonym for the title

Puppies
cuddly and cute
chewing, playing, barking
falling asleep under the bed
True friends

CINQUAIN
Whole Group

Puppies
cuddly and cute
chewing, playing, barking
falling asleep under the bed
True friends

_____

_____

_____

_____

_____

ACROSTICQUINCLERIHEW

CINQUAIN
Independent

Use this page to organize your ideas into the web with the subject in a circle at the center. Write descriptive words and actions in circles around the center. Then write your own cinquain on the lines below. The syllable pattern is provided for you.

Line 1: 2-syllable subject
Line 2: 4 syllables that describe subject
Line 3: 6 syllables that express action relating to subject
Line 4: 8 syllables that express feeling or an observation
Line 5: 2 syllables that rename the subject

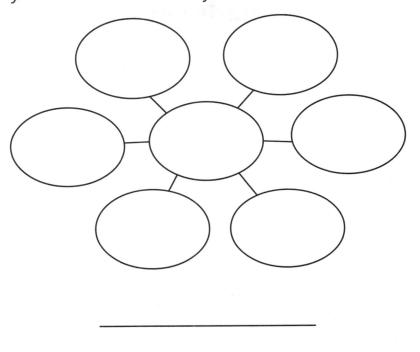

_____

_____

_____

_____

_____

Rigby Best Teachers Press

CLERIHEW

Background

This four-line rhymed poem is named for its creator, British detective writer Edmund Clerihew Bentley (1875-1956). The clerihew is a good-humored poem about a famous person.

The clerihew is a formula poem with a set pattern but no predetermined number of syllables or words per line. The formula is in its rhyme pattern. It consists of two rhymed couplets (an *a a b b* pattern). After introducing the name of the individual being recognized, the three remaining lines are used to provide a brief glimpse of that person's life and accomplishments or to celebrate some special talent or attribute that the person may possess. The challenge in writing a clerihew is that the celebrity's name must be at the end of the first line and the next line must rhyme with it.

Remarkable Maya Angelou,
Writer, poet, and teacher, too,
She speaks with fire and gentle grace,
She makes the world a better place.

Michelangelo
born long, long ago.
Lay on his back to paint a ceiling,
which, centuries later, is still appealing.

Brilliant man was ole Abe Lincoln,
Short on schooling, long on thinkin'
Brought emancipation, braved the Civil War,
The Gettysburg Address his finest hour.

CLERIHEW
Whole Group

Brilliant man was ole Abe Lincoln,
Short on schooling, long on thinkin'
Brought emancipation, braved the Civil War,
The Gettysburg Address his finest hour.

Rigby Best Teachers Press

CLERIHEW
Independent

It is a good idea to brainstorm ideas about the person's life before writing a clerihew. Include the most interesting aspects of the person's life–something that would stand out or is well-known. Remember that clerihews are intended to poke fun gently. Never write something unkind about a person.

Rhyme Pattern:

Line 1: person's name
Line 2: rhymes with line 1
Line 3: fact about person's life
Line 4: rhymes with line 3

_____

_____

_____

_____

Check to see if your clerihew is the best it can be.

❑ Your clerihew should have two couplets that rhyme.
❑ It should have rhythm or a beat when you read it aloud.
❑ It should be playful, not unkind.

CONCRETE POEM
Background

Concrete poems are also called shape poems. The Ancient Greeks called this form of writing a calligram. It utilizes words, letters, type size, and space in a unique way. Some people say this is not truly poetry because it doesn't have rhythm or any other poetic elements. However it does have a physical arrangement on the page that conveys meaning and asks the reader to take a closer look. Other concrete poems suggest movement by organizing the words in a stair-step or waterfall formation.

In any form of poetry, words should be well chosen and used sparingly. This is especially true for concrete poems because only enough words to form an outline of an object are used. When the words are arranged as though they are traveling in a particular direction they convey movement or action with only one or two words. In the case of concrete poems that form the actual shape of an object, words must be chosen with great care so that a single word does not cause that line to interrupt the integrity of the intended shape.

While most poetry is meant to be read aloud, concrete poetry communicates through the visual arrangement of words on paper. This adds another dimension to concrete poems.

In creating a concrete outline poem, it's a good idea to sketch lightly (with a pencil) the object's outline so that words can be written along that line to form the poem. When composing a concrete poem with an actual shape, drawing the form lightly or cutting paper in the shape of the form will ensure that its borders are kept intact. Concrete poetry that uses words to suggest movement or action is more effective if the type of motion (vertical, horizontal, or circular) is related to the theme of the poem.

golden delicious always nutritious cameo and gala red try a jonagold instead fuji makes a tasty treat granny smith is good to eat. braeburn, pink lady, winesap, or rome; bring lots of apples into your home

CONCRETE POEM
Whole Group

Flying
high above
the world in the
blue sky. The clouds around
me whisper stay up here. Do
not sail down to the
ground below. This
is the perfect
place to
be.

ACROSTIC QUAIN CLERIHEW

CONCRETE POEM
Independent

Think about a simple shape that interests you: a butterfly, a basketball, a boat, the sun, a tree, and so on.

Use the space below to write words or phrases you associate with that object. Draw the object on a scrap piece of paper several times to practice placing the words within the shape. Use the framed space below for your final composition.

_____

_____

_____

DIAMANTE
Background

This type of poem is arranged in the shape of a diamond. It helps students apply what they know about opposites and parts of speech. A diamante provides them with an opportunity to study how words relate to one another outside the context of a sentence or paragraph. For example, if the words used on the first and last lines of a diamante are cat and dog, student poets are challenged to find words that describe and define each species using those attributes that are in contrast with one another. (Both cats and dogs are furry, so that adjective would not be a good choice to describe one or the other).

Line 1: one word (noun)
Line 2: two words (adjectives)
Line 3: three words (verbs ending in "ing")
Line 4: four words (nouns)
Line 5: three words (verbs ending in "ing")
Line 6: two words (adjectives)
Line 7: one word (noun)

Trick
nasty, sneaky
plotting, scheming, planning
prank, joke, reward, surprise
giving, sharing, enjoying
sweet, tasty
Treat

Ice
solid, slippery
skating, sliding, gliding
pond, lake, river, ocean
swimming, floating, splashing
liquid, wet
water

Trick
nasty, sneaky
plotting, scheming, planning
prank, joke, reward, surprise
giving, sharing, enjoying
sweet, tasty
Treat

_____

_____ _____

_____ _____ _____

_____ _____ _____ _____

_____ _____ _____

_____ _____

_____

DIAMANTE

Independent

To write an interesting diamante, start with two words that seem like opposites. These become the theme of your poem. Find the common adjectives or verbs that tie them together. Your poem may influence people to look at these opposites in a new way. Use the lines below to write your diamante.

Line 1: one noun
Line 2: two adjectives that describe line 1
Line 3: three verbs that end in "ing" that describe line 1
Line 4: four nouns, first two refer to line 1 and the next two nouns refer to line 7
Line 5: three verbs that end in "ing" that describe line 7
Line 6: two adjectives that describe line 7
Line 7: one noun that is the opposite of line 1

_____

_____ _____

_____ _____ _____

_____ _____ _____ _____

_____ _____ _____

_____ _____

_____

FOUND POEM
Background

Found poetry is based on the fascinating idea that within literary prose there exists wonderful poetic moments. A found poem is created by carefully reading a few pages from a book, magazine, or newspaper, and selecting words or phrases that convey poetic elements. The words are then copied onto slips of paper. As the words and phrases are moved around they take on poetic cadence and imagery. Once the found poem sounds right, it should be written and given a title. A fun alternative is to allow students to cut the words out of magazines and arrange the cut out pieces.

Some may argue that found poems are not true poetry. The process of creating these poems, however, does allow readers to look more critically at what they are reading and enhances their appreciation of language. As students search newspaper and magazine articles, textbooks, and fictional paperbacks for poetic language, they become the ultimate editors of verse.

Explorers

Great adventures
in the distance
On the horizon
sailors, pirates
whales and ships.
That would be exciting!

Nite Tale

SOME magic
or mischief
cloudless night,
Ceiling of stars
telling a story
solitude, untouched
Any moment now
I must go.

Remind students to bring in magazines and newspapers.

FOUND POEM
Whole Group

Nite Tale

SOME magic
or mischief
cloudless night,
Ceiling of stars
telling **a** story
solitude, untouched
Any moment now
I must **go.**

_____

_____

_____

_____

_____

_____

FOUND POEM
Independent

To write a found poem you must have an abundance of words. Start by collecting magazines, newspapers, and all types of books. Find an article or chapter of a book that seems like an interesting source for poetry. Read carefully, perhaps more than once, looking for words that catch your attention – maybe a word you don't know or just like the sound of. Use index cards, cut in half, to copy the words or phrases that you like. Rearrange the card pieces until the order takes on a poetic sound. When the found poem sounds right to you, write it on the lines below and give it a title.

_____

_____

_____

_____

_____

_____

_____

_____

_____

HAIKU
Background

Haiku, the most familiar word-count poetry, originated in Japan. A haiku contains 17 syllables, divided into three unrhymed lines. This poetic form captures a single vivid image of nature in a single moment. Haiku presents a pair of contrasting images that, together, evoke mood and emotion. One image suggests time and place, while the other is an intense but momentary observation.

In order to write an effective haiku poem, student poets must choose their words with great care since the word-count format limits the number of syllables they can use to express their vision of a natural object.

The brief length of haiku prompted many poets to have their work illustrated as a way of underscoring the image created by the 17 syllables. Other poets grouped several haiku poems together to form a collection, celebrating a particular aspect of nature—flowers, winter, or dawn, for example.

Although student poems may differ slightly, the prescribed formula for a haiku poem is listed below:

Line 1: 5 syllables
Line 2: 7 syllables
Line 3: 5 syllables

Birds in the treetops
merrily chirping their songs
nature's gentle hearts.

Autumn leaves crunching
beneath our feet, walking home
on this crisp fall day.

Pond water rippling,
the stone breaks into its depth,
falling on soft sand.

Pond water rippling,
the stone breaks into its depth,
falling on soft sand.

_____

_____

_____

HAIKU
Independent

Once you have selected a topic for your haiku, it's a good idea to write down several words that convey something about that topic. Then, narrow your list to the words that evoke the strongest imagery. Think of a scene in nature and imagine you are taking a picture. What would your photograph capture? The sights, sounds, colors, and actions all become imagery for your haiku.

Use the lines below for writing some haiku.

Haiku pattern
Line 1: 5 syllables
Line 2: 7 syllables
Line 3: 5 syllables

_____   _____

_____   _____

_____   _____

_____

_____

_____

Check to be sure your haikus are the best they can be.

❏ Each haiku should have 17 syllables in three lines.
❏ The haikus should focus on nature.
❏ They should be written to capture a single moment.

LIMERICK

Background

This light form of verse makes use of rhyme and rhythm. It is believed that limericks originated in the town of Limerick, Ireland, during the 19th century. They are humorous poems that are often bold or bawdy.

Limerick is easy to recognize in that you can hear a regular rhythm, a repeated pattern of stressed and unstressed syllables throughout the poem and from line to line. This regular repeated pattern is referred to as meter. The word *meter* comes from the Greek root meaning "measure." The two most commonly measured elements are the number of syllables per line, and the number of stressed syllables per line. Both syllables and stresses are commonly analyzed by means of a unit called the foot.

Limericks have a definite pattern of anapestic feet in five lines.
anapestic: da da **dum** (unstressed, unstressed, stressed) = 1 metrical foot

Line 1: three metrical feet a   (da da **dum**, da da **dum**, da da **dum**)
Line 2: three metrical feet a
Line 3: two metrical feet   b
Line 4: two metrical feet   b
Line 5: three metrical feet a

Disguise

There once was a lady called Maggie,
Whose dog was enormous and shaggy,
The front end of him
Looked vicious and grim
But the back end was friendly and waggy.

Anonymous

Limericks are recited with a wide variation in vocal inflection considered "sing-song" in nature. This helps reflect the light-heartedness of most limericks. It is a good idea to read several limericks to a class of student poets before instructing them to write a limerick of their own. You may also want to encourage students to compose limericks in groups.

Disguise

There once was a lady called Maggie,
Whose dog was enormous and shaggy,
The front end of him
Looked vicious and grim
But the back end was friendly and waggy.

Anonymous

LIMERICK
Independent

Writing your own limerick is not difficult–it is actually fun–however certain guidelines must be followed. Limericks have a rhyme pattern (as shown below) but more importantly, each line has a definite rhythm. Reading limericks aloud is the best way to become familiar with the way they sound, so be sure you have many examples to read. Sometimes the best way to get started is to start with the classic limerick opener:

There once was a lady (man) from...

Use the pattern as a guide for composing your own limerick on the lines below.

Line 1: three metrical feet   a   (da da **dum**, da da **dum**, da da **dum**)
Line 2: three metrical feet   a
Line 3: two metrical feet   b
Line 4: two metrical feet   b
Line 5: three metrical feet   a

_____

_____

_____

_____

_____

Of course the true test of a limerick is to read it aloud and listen to how it sounds. Read it aloud with a partner.

❏ Does it have the right rhythm?
❏ Does it make you smile?

TANKA
Background

This less familiar form of Japanese syllable-count verse consists of five lines with a total of 31 syllables. Tanka is often regarded as a longer form of haiku since it most often deals with nature themes. What makes tanka different is that, unlike haiku, it does include poetic elements such as simile, metaphor, and personification. As student poets develop some proficiency in writing haiku, they may wish to explore the longer form of tanka in order to include more imagery in their compositions.

Both haiku and tanka can be used effectively with science instruction as students find elements of nature interesting. They can use these short poetic forms to share their enthusiasm with the rest of the group. Like haiku, tanka poems can be greatly enhanced when illustrations are added.

Tanka pattern:
Line 1: 5 syllables
Line 2: 7 syllables
Line 3: 5 syllables
Line 4: 7 syllables
Line 5: 7 syllables

Ice Cream Cone

It drips onto the
scorching sidewalk from my arm
splashing my new shoes.
I don't mind that it's melting,
day one, summer vacation.

Ice Cream Cone

It drips onto the
scorching sidewalk from my arm
splashing my new shoes.
I don't mind that it's melting,
day one, summer vacation.

_____

_____

_____

_____

TANKA
Independent

Planning to write tanka is a lot like planning to write haiku since it also focuses on nature themes. Use the same strategy of thinking of a scene as a photograph. But add a new dimension. Try to determine the mood of the scene. Is it upbeat and excited or calm and tranquil? Include simile, metaphor, or personification to convey feeling in your tanka. Think of how you write sentences. You just start writing and the words come to you. You can try this as a way of getting started. Compose a short story. Then go back and choose the important words that fit the syllable pattern. Use the lines below for writing your tanka.

Line 1: 5 syllables
Line 2: 7 syllables
Line 3: 5 syllables
Line 4: 7 syllables
Line 5: 7 syllables

_____

_____

_____

_____

_____

SONNET
Background

A sonnet is a lyric poem of 14 lines with a formal rhyme scheme. It expresses different aspects of a single thought, mood, or feeling, sometimes resolved or summed up in the last lines of the poem.

The two main forms of the sonnet are the Italian (Petrarchan) and the English (Shakespearean) popularized by William Shakespeare. The English sonnet is divided into three quatrains and one couplet, each rhyming differently. The first quatrain presents the theme, while the second and third develop it. The final couplet brings the sonnet to an effective close. In the 16th century the English sonnet dealt primarily with the subject of love. In the 17th century the sonnet tradition continued, but with varied subject matter. As free verse increased in popularity, the specific formula and rhyme pattern of the sonnet fell out of style. Today, however, Shakespeare's sonnets remain one of the most widely read and appreciated forms of poetry.

The longer length and more detailed formula of the sonnet makes it a likely topic of study for middle school students. While it is not essential that they follow such a precise rhyming pattern with their own compositions, the sonnet formula presents an interesting challenge for student poets.

XVIII

Line 1: a   Shall I compare thee to a summer's day?
Line 2: b   Thou art more lovely and more temperate:
Line 3: a   Rough winds do shake the darling buds of May,
Line 4: b   And summer's lease hath all too short a date:
Line 5: c   Sometime too hot the eye of heaven shines,
Line 6: d   And often is his gold complexion dimm'd,
Line 7: c   And every fair from fair sometime declines,
Line 8: d   By chance, or nature's changing course untrimm'd
Line 9: e   But thy eternal summer shall not fade,
Line 10: f   Nor lose possession of that fair thou ow'st,
Line 11: e   Nor shall death brag thou wander'st in his shade,
Line 12: f   When in eternal lines to time thou grow'st,
Line 13: g   So long as men can breathe, or eyes can see,
Line 14: g   So long lives this, and this gives life to thee.

–William Shakespeare

SONNET

Background

Sonnets use 14 lines to develop a theme. Each set of 4 lines is called a quatrain and the last pair of lines is a couplet. In traditional sonnets each line contains ten syllables. The rhyme pattern is fairly predictable until the final two (indented) lines that rhyme with one another rather than with a previous set of lines. The rhyming pattern is as follows:

Line 1   a
Line 2   b
Line 3   a
Line 4   b   This quatrain states the theme.
_____

Line 5   c
Line 6   d
Line 7   c
Line 8   d   This quatrain develops the theme.
_____

Line 9   e
Line 10   f
Line 11   e   This quatrain further develops the theme or expresses
Line 12   f   conflict.
_____

Line 13   g
Line 14   g   This couplet unifies the whole and provides a climax.

The next page has been designed for writing a sonnet. The lines are numbered and letters representing the rhyme scheme have been provided at the end of each line.

 For both the sonnet and the ballad it is recommended that you complete the whole-group pages as a shared writing lesson so as not to create a high level of anxiety and frustration for students.

SONNET
Whole Group

_____

1 _____ a

2 _____ b

3 _____ a

4 _____ b

5 _____ c

6 _____ d

7 _____ c

8 _____ d

9 _____ e

10 _____ f

11 _____ e

12 _____ f

13 _____ g

14 _____ g

BALLAD
Background

Ballads are stories about famous people or events, told in short stanzas—a small group of theme-related lines within a poem separated by a space or, sometimes, by a refrain. In most cases, ballads contain a specific rhyme pattern, (*a b a b* or *a a b b*) but may also be arranged in a free verse form.

Each stanza in a ballad contains related information about a person's life or about an important event. The stanzas of a ballad are arranged in chronological order so that the story unfolds in a logical sequence. Because of the nature of its content, the ballad can easily be incorporated into a social studies lesson.

The refrain of a ballad is usually shorter than the stanza (2–4 lines in length) and is repeated throughout the ballad. The refrain might be used to create a particular visual image of that event. It is important to note that many well-known ballads do not contain refrains as they are not necessary to the style.

Ballads have their origins in songs written about significant events or people. The author of the ballad contributes something to a culture's popular heritage as the song is passed from generation to generation. Many ballads written in North America recount the journeys and exploits of this country's early inhabitants. They covered a range of subjects from historical figures like Davy Crockett or fictional characters such as Paul Bunyan. European ballads tell stories of royalty or cultural heroes like Robin Hood. Reading and writing ballads provides an entertaining way for students to examine the past of their homeland and the homelands of others.

Henry Wadsworth Longfellow wrote some famous ballads including "Excelsior," "Paul Revere's Ride," and "The Wreck of the Hesperus." The ballad "The Village Blacksmith" is another example by Longfellow, praising the virtues of a less notable character.

The Village Blacksmith

Under a spreading chestnut-tree
The village smithy stands;
The smith, a mighty man is he,
With large and sinewy hands;
And the muscles of his brawny arms
Are strong as iron bands.

His hair is crisp, and black, and long,
His face is like the tan;
His brow is wet with honest sweat,
He earns whate'er he can,
And looks the whole world in the face,
For he owes not any man.

Week in, week out, from morn till night,
You can hear his bellows blow;
You can hear him swing his heavy sledge,
With measured beat and slow,
Like a sexton ringing the village bell,
When the evening sun is low.

And children coming home from school
Look in at the open door;
They love to see the flaming forge,
And hear the bellows roar,
And catch the burning sparks that fly
Like chaff from a threshing-floor.

BALLAD
Background

He goes on Sunday to the church,
And sits among his boys;
He hears the parson pray and preach,
He hears his daughter's voice,
Singing in the village choir,
And it makes his heart rejoice.

It sounds to him like her mother's voice,
Singing in Paradise!
He needs must think of her once more,
How in the grave she lies;
And with his hard, rough hand he wipes
A tear out of his eyes.

Toiling,–rejoicing,–sorrowing,
Onward through life he goes;
Each morning sees some task begin,
Each evening sees it close;
Something attempted, something done,
Has earned a night's repose.

Thanks, thanks to thee, my worthy friend,
For the lesson thou hast taught!
Thus at the flaming forge of life
Our fortunes must be wrought;
Thus on its sounding anvil shaped
Each burning deed and thought.

— *Henry Wadsworth Longfellow*

BALLAD
Whole Group

The topic for your ballad should be a person or event that you are interested in. You do not have to choose a famous person. Maybe you know someone who has done something exceptional or is important to you and you want your ballad to be a celebration of him or her.

Writing a ballad is a lot like plotting a story. The reader must know whom it is about and what is happening. Use the graphic organizer below to prepare your ideas for the ballad.

Main Character

Setting

Supporting Characters

Conflict

Turning Point

Details

Details

Details

Resolution

Use the lines provided on the next page to compose a ballad.

Rigby Best Teachers Press

BALLAD
Whole Group

The Ballad of _____

By

_____

_____

_____

_____

_____

_____

_____

_____

_____

Section 3:
Using Poetry Across the Curriculum

There are many ways to involve students in creating poetry outside the language arts curriculum. The activities in this section are a sample of what can be done once student poets have explored the basics of poetry and feel confident to use it as a means of expressing themselves and what they know about the world around them.

The Internet has many sites devoted to poetry. Specific sites for children's poetry are rich with activities, lessons, and examples for you to print and use. A list of particularly good ones is provided for your convenience.

www.kidstory.com/poetry.html
Read other students' poetry and publish poetry online.

www.veeceet.com
Read lots of silly poetry.

www.gigglepoetry.com
Read and rate poetry. Activities and poetry class.

www.poetryteachers.com
Poetry class, poetry theater, and poetry contests.

home.earthlink.net/~froggie1/index.html
Children's author's poetry site.

www.yahooligans.com/School Bell/Language Arts/Poetry
Read and listen to poetry.

Note: All of these sites have been previewed at the time of this printing to ensure that the content and links are appropriate for educational purposes and contain no offensive materials. However, Rigby is not responsible for the content of any website listed in this book, except their own website. All material on other sites is the responsibility of the hosts and creators.

The Shape of Things to Come

Curriculum Area: Science

Purpose: To express ideas related to an invention or natural phenomena

Poetic Form: Concrete poem

Activity:

After exploring various inventions in science class, instruct students to select an invention and brainstorm for words and phrases that are related to it. Ask students to think of how the invention affects the five senses, as well as its impact on the world. Have them list these words and phrases, grouping them by length, on a separate sheet of paper. Next, give students a sheet of drawing paper to sketch a light outline of the invention. They should then arrange the related words and phrases to form a more visible outline of the topic. Another method is to place the words and phrases in varying lengths inside the outline to form a concrete shape of the object.

This activity works equally well for natural phenomena studied in earth science, such as rainstorms or blizzards. The words could be arranged on the page to represent the phenomenon's movement. (Raindrops, wind gusts, or tornadoes).

 Students' concrete poetry makes a great bulletin board display.

From A to Z

Curriculum Area: Science

Purpose: To use rhyme while demonstrating knowledge of a topic

Poetic Form: Rhyming poem

Activity:

After studying a unit in science, brainstorm words related to the unit that begin with each letter of the alphabet. Write these on an overhead or chalkboard. Accept more ideas than are needed so that there will be more of a selection available when the poem is being composed. Next, divide the class into small groups. Instruct each group to compose a 26-line rhyming poem using the alphabetized topic words from the brainstorming session. The group may choose their own rhyme pattern such as *a b a b* or *a a b b*, or any other pattern they decide.

A is for astronauts, real space pioneers,	a
B is for back-up, so there'll be no fear,	a
C is for comet, a fast-moving star,	b
D is for distance, measure with a light year.	a

Student can group a few lines, or a couplet, on each page. They can then add illustrations to make an ABC rhyming book for the science unit.

 ABC rhyming books make an excellent addition to the class library.

Nature's Diamonds

Curriculum Area: Science—For every action, there is an equal and opposite reaction.

Purpose: To examine opposites found in nature

Poetic Form: Diamante

Activity:

Discuss, as a class, opposites found in nature, such as mountains and valleys or sunrise and sunset. Encourage students to look beyond obvious choices for more complex opposites. Instruct students, working in pairs, to select a pair of opposites and list the attributes of each in separate columns, focusing on physical descriptions and related activities. Then, instruct each pair to write a diamante for their opposites.

Before displaying the completed poems in the classroom, ask each pair to read their diamante to the rest of the class, stopping before reading Line 7. Challenge the class to use the first term and the descriptions of both opposites to guess the second opposite.

Sing a Song of Science

Curriculum Area: Science

Purpose: To explain scientific processes in correct sequence

Poetic Form: Song

Activity:

After studying a particular process like photosynthesis or cell division in science class, list the steps involved on the board or overhead. Assign each step to a small group.

Have students work in small groups to compose a rhyme couplet that tells about one of the steps. Couplets can then be paired to form a four-line stanza. These will be the verses.

Next, as a whole class, compose a couplet that identifies the process and tells about it. This will be the refrain.

Now, with groups offering their stanzas orally, combine all the verses, in order, on the board. Use the refrain to separate the verses.

Have students copy the completed song so they will each have a copy. Ask them to think of a popular song's tune that might go with the rhythm of the song. If an existing tune does not go well with it, maybe a student could compose music for the song.

   The song would make a great review for a test.

Who Am I?

Curriculum Area: Social Studies

Purpose: To create a sketch of a famous person

Poetic Form: Riddle

Activity:

Write the names of several historical figures on separate slips of paper, placing them in a bowl. Let each student pick one name, then ask them to write a riddle about that figure. Have children utilize library sources to gather information. The trick to writing an effective riddle is using information that distinguishes that person from everyone else but remains vague enough to be a challenge to solve. It is not necessary for riddles to have a rhyme pattern but it is acceptable. When the riddles are complete, post them on a class bulletin board, numbering each one. Give students a set period of time–one day/week–to solve as many of the riddles as they can. Encourage the student to utilize a variety of reference materials such as encyclopedias, the Internet, and textbooks.

**Our symbol
of freedom
was stitched long ago.
The stars
and stripes
is the flag
that she sewed.**

The Ballad of a Famous Person

Curriculum Area: Social Studies

Purpose: To recount, in logical sequence, events in a famous person's life

Poetic Form: Ballad

Have examples of ballads about historical figures available before beginning this activity.

Activity:

Have students work in small groups to select a historical figure and list some of his or her accomplishments. Next, have students arrange the events in chronological order, selecting the most interesting ones. Explain to student groups that they will use the information they have gathered to compose a ballad. While a rhyme pattern is not required, ballads do contain a specific rhythm pattern, which can be observed by reading or singing popular ballads aloud. Add student-composed music, or use the tune of a popular song, to accompany the words and have each group perform their ballad for the rest of the class.

It's a Celebration!

Curriculum Area: Social Studies

Purpose: To examine various holiday customs observed by other cultures

Poetic Form: Various

Activity:
While studying the customs of a particular group of people (or during a holiday season), assign students to research various customs associated with an upcoming holiday observed in another country or in this country during another time period. Have them use the information in a holiday-inspired poem. Another variation of this activity would be to have each student pretend to be a historical figure such as George Washington or Martin Luther King, Jr., and write a poem about the upcoming holiday from that person's point of view. For example, a poem composed by George Washington describing how he led American troops across the Delaware River.

"A" is for America

Curriculum Area: Social Studies

Purpose: To identify symbols associated with a person, place, or event

Poetic Form: Acrostic poem

Activity:

While exploring a social studies unit, instruct each student to select a person, place, or event from that unit. Encourage students to gather information from sources beyond the textbook. Next, have each student write an acrostic poem using all or part of the name as the title. Review the form of an acrostic poem before beginning.

Completed acrostics make an excellent bulletin board display.

Amos, the Alliterative Alligator

Curriculum Area: Language Arts/Spelling

Purpose: To practice alliteration and spelling

Poetic Form: Alliteration

Activity:

Have students list words from past and present spelling lists that have the same beginning sounds, reminding them that the same beginning letter does not insure that the sounds will be the same. Assign students to work in pairs, asking them to select several words with the same beginning letter. Then, have each pair use all the words that have the same beginning sound to write a short 1–2 line alliterative poem. Remind them that rhyming is optional. They may use small connecting words, such as *the* or *and,* but the rest of the words in the poem should begin with the same sound.

Dear Poet

Curriculum Area: Creative Writing

Purpose: To express appreciation of poetry from a published author

Poetic Form: Various

Activity:

Encourage students to express their respect for a particular poet's work by writing to authors. Instead of writing letters in a traditional format, have students collect several examples of their favorite poet's work, then compose a poem using that poet's format. Within the poem, the student may talk about their favorite poems or why they enjoy the work of that poet. Brainstorm beforehand the types of things students could include in their letters before they begin composing their own poems. Contact publishing companies to determine where mail to a particular poet should be addressed. The most sincere form of flattery is imitation, and the published poets will, no doubt, be gratified by the students' imitation of their writing style.

Character Study

Curriculum Area: Literature / Language Arts

Purpose: To create profile of a story character (traits, talents, achievements)

Poetic Form: Ballad

Activity:

Everybody has a story–even the characters who live, work, play, and dream in fictional settings. Young readers return to certain books on the strength of their attachment to these characters. As students demonstrate a preference for certain fictional characters, give them the opportunity to share their enthusiasm with classmates by writing a tribute to that character. Just as poets compose *ballads* to commemorate the lives and times of famous people and popular legends, students can capture the spirit of fictional characters using this same poetic form. After students have selected their favorite fictional character, instruct them to brainstorm about that character's life, highlighting their talents and accomplishments. Examine some published *ballads* to get an idea of how these compositions are organized. After the *ballad* is complete, encourage students to add music (student composed or previously published) to their composition before sharing it with the rest of the class.

Scenes from a Poem

Curriculum Area: Art

Purpose: To create visual montages that reflect the emotions of a poem

Poetic Form: Various

Activity:

Instruct each student to select one of their own poems or a work from a published poet. After reading the poem two or three times, students should be able to focus on visual images that come to mind. Ask students to collect images to accompany the poem from photographs, drawings, or magazines. Have students create a montage on posterboard to display their selected images. After students have created a montage, they can share the images with classmates during an oral reading of the poem.

Section 4:
Instant Poetry

Involving students in poetry on a regular basis is an effective way to develop genuine interest in the genre. The challenge remains in creating and executing response activities that are meaningful and entertaining experiences. Exercises that call on students to make connections between poetry and their lives are most likely to have a long-term effect on their opinion of poetry. Varying the length and type of activities increases the chances of tapping into each student's creativity.

In addition to including poetry in all areas of the curriculum, it's a good idea to develop poetry mini-lessons associated with holidays, upcoming classroom and school events, or students' personal interests. In this way, students will identify poetry with positive experiences, increasing the possibility that they will see poetry as a valid means of self-expression.

The exercises in this section are designed for maximum student involvement and interest with a minimum of teacher preparation. They can be included in a larger, more structured poetry unit or used to reinforce poetic forms already studied. The objective of these activities is to involve students with poetry in an easy-to-do format, while fostering enjoyment and appreciation for this genre.

Name _____ Date _____

Riddle Rhyme

A riddle describes something common in a roundabout way. Have you ever heard the riddle, "What is black and white and red all over?" Of course, there are a variety of answers, and that is what makes guessing so much fun. There is always the possibility that the reader or listener will be caught off guard.

◆ Think of a simple object.
◆ Write a 4–6 line riddle to describe it.
◆ You can make your riddle rhyme, but it does not have to.
◆ Be sure to include enough clues so classmates will be able to guess what is being described.

Example:

**What are shiny and bright,
and can sometimes over bite?
There are usually 32,
that do their best to chew.**

What Am I?

_____

_____

_____

_____

Name _____ Date _____

Introducing the One and Only . . .

How would you describe your best friend? We often see our friends in a unique way. We see their gifts and talents and the traits that make them special.

◆ Write the letters of your friend's name, vertically, on the short lines at the left side of the page.
◆ Use the rest of each line to write an acrostic poem about him or her.
◆ Include hobbies or favorite things and character traits.

_____ _____

_____ _____

_____ _____

_____ _____

_____ _____

_____ _____

Poetry
Just add imagination
RIDDLE RHYME TIME TO RHYME BEING ME

Name ______________________________ Date __________

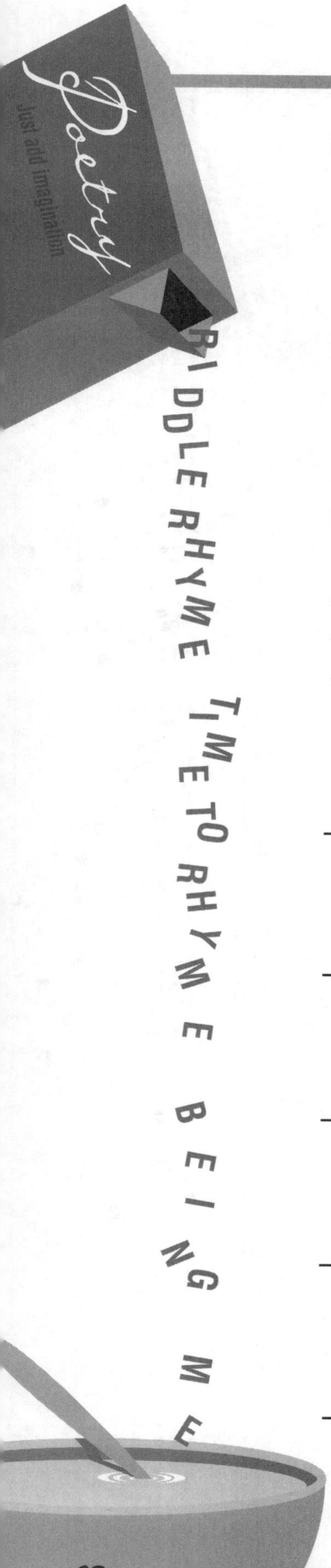

Hilarious Homograph-a-phones

Homographs are words that look alike but are pronounced differently and have different meaning; for example, "I *read* that book last year, but I want to *read* it again."

Homophones are words that look different and have different meanings but sound the same; for example, "The *hair* on that *hare* is brown."

- Think of several pairs of homographs and homophones.
- Use pairs of homographs or homophones in the same sentence.
- Combine 2–4 of the sentences to form a poem.

____

____

____

____

____

Name _____   Date _____

It's Time to Rhyme

◆ Work in a group of four students.

◆ Think of four words that rhyme with one another and write each word on separate index cards.

◆ Each person in the group must take one card and compose a line that ends with the word.

◆ Then, work together to combine and arrange the lines each person wrote to form a poem.

◆ Write the poem your group composed on the lines below.

_____

_____

_____

_____

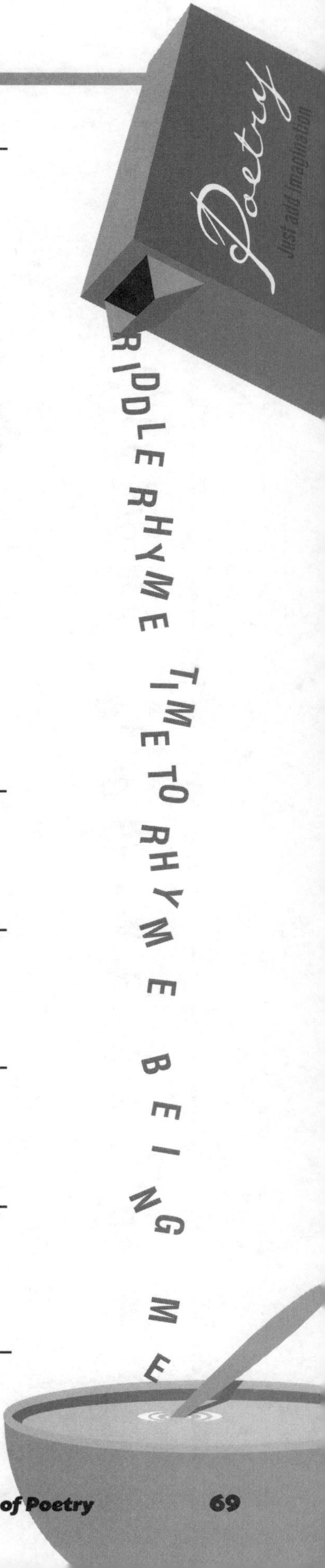

RIDDLE RHYME TIME TO RHYME BEING ME

Name _____ Date _____

A Clerihew for You

A *clerihew* is a four-lined rhyming poem that describes a person. The first line always ends with the person's name. The rhyme pattern is *a a b b*.

Work with a partner to compose *clerihews* about each other.
Highlight the traits or talents of one another.

_____

_____

_____

_____

Name _____ Date _____

Think Hink-Pink

A hink-pink is made up of two 1-syllable rhyming words (pail sale).
A hinky-pinky is made up of two 2-syllable rhyming words (dairy ferry).
A hinkity-pinkity is made up of two 3-syllable rhyming words (antelope cantaloupe).

These pairs usually answer a riddle or describe something. For example, a *pail sale* can be thought of as a bucket clearance, and a *dairy ferry* is a milk boat.

◆ First, think of a rhyme pair, and then think of a way to describe it.
◆ Follow the syllable count for each one.
◆ After writing your hink-pinks, read them to a partner and see if you can guess each other's, based on the description.

Hink-Pink _____

_____

Hinky-Pinky _____

_____

Hinkity-Pinkity _____

_____

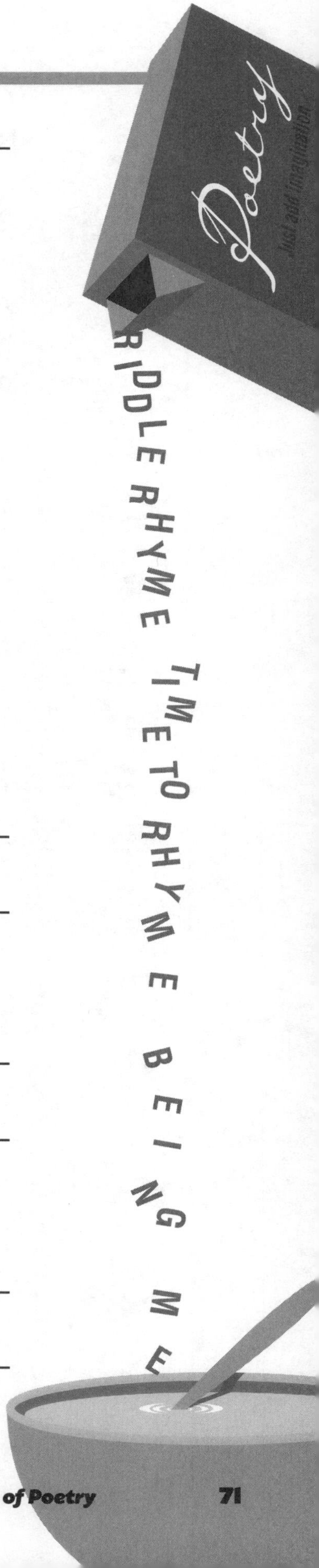

RIDDLE RHYME TIME TO RHYME BEING ME

Poetry
Just add Imagination

RIDDLE RHYME TIME TO RHYME BEING ME

Name _____ Date _____

Diamante for Two

A diamante is a 7-line poem that compares opposite noun pairs. The first half of the poem describes the first word in the pair while the second half of the poem describes the other word.

◆ Use the lines below to write the first half of a *diamante*, stopping at the asterisk.
◆ Then, switch this paper with a partner.
◆ While your partner completes your *diamante*, you supply the final half of their poem.
◆ Meet with you partner to discuss the completed poems.

1 Noun   _____

2 Adjectives _____   _____

3 "ing" verbs _____   _____   _____

2 Nouns _____   _____ * _____   _____ 2 Nouns

3 "ing" verbs _____   _____   _____

2 Adjectives _____   _____

1 Noun   _____

Name _____ Date _____

Color Me a Rainbow

What do you think of when you see the color *yellow*? How does *blue* taste? When do you feel like *purple*? How does *pink* sound? What smells remind you of *green*?

◆ Use all five of your senses to write this poem about any color.
◆ Write the color on the first line.

_____

Sounds like _____

Tastes like _____

Feels like _____

Looks like _____

Smells like _____

Tomorrow and Today

The word, *tomorrow*, is full of promise and unfulfilled dreams. The word, *today*, is somewhere to be until that time comes. Everyone has ideas of what he or she wants to do and where he or she wants to be, but for now, we're here. The poem activity below uses the poetic element of repetition.

◆ In the spaces below, complete the sentences about tomorrow and today.
◆ You can choose to add more tomorrow and today lines.

Tomorrow, I want to _____

but for today, I guess I'll _____

Tomorrow, I want to _____

but for today, I guess I'll _____

Tomorrow, I want to _____

but for today, I guess I'll _____

RIDDLE RHYME TIME TO RHYME BEING ME

Name _____ Date _____

Being Me

The best thing about poetry is that it comes in all shapes and sizes. Some poetry is made up of long, flowing phrases while other poems have only one or two words on each line. Poetry can be about happy times or sad memories. It can be about things that move us or about nothing at all. Some poems rhyme, others don't. Some poems paint a picture with words, others use the words to form a shape or outline. The only thing about poetry that never changes is that it is *always* changing.

◆ On the lines below, pick your favorite kind of poem and write a poem celebrating you.

_____

_____

_____

_____

_____

Bibliography

Shakespeare, William, *Sonnet XVII*, in *The Riverside Shakespeare*, edited by G. Blakemore Evan, Boston: Houghton Mifflin, 1974.

Longfellow, Henry Wadsworth, "The Village Blacksmith" in *The Oxford Book of Children's Verse in America*, edited by Donald Hall, Oxford University Press, 1985.